This book was
donated by
**Sarah and Drew
Snyder**

April 2008

Charles Wright Academy
Lower School Library
7723 Chambers Creek Road West
University Place, WA 98467

MOONSNACKS

A N D   A S S O R T E D   N U T S

MOONSNACKS

Someone ate the Moon last night
And left only a crest,
I wonder if he'll come tonight
And eat up all the rest?
I wonder if it tasted like
A great, big cheese balloon?
Do you suppose somehow last night
A mouse got on the Moon?

GREENE BARK PRESS, INC.
P.O. Box 1108
Bridgeport, CT 06601-1108

POEMS BY MARY GRACE DEMBECK
ILLUSTRATIONS BY JEAN PIDGEON

ISBN 1-880851-11-3

Published by Greene Bark Press Inc.
P.O. Box 1108
Bridgeport, CT 06601-1108

CONTENTS

GADZOOK TEA

A witch, feeling lonely for company,
Invited some neighbors to come at three,
She made Lizard Scones
And Tart Jelly Bones,
And brewed a big cauldron of Gadzook Tea.

Her door gong sounded, she shrieked with glee,
There, on her stair, stood her company,
A dragon, two rats,
Three snakes and four bats,
Five spiders, six toads and a chimpanzee.

"Creep in!", cried the witch, "You are right on time...
I just finished boiling a bucket of slime,
To go with my scones
And Tart Jelly Bones!"
"Oh, good!", hissed a snake, "They're all favorites of mine!"

They crawled and they crept to their usual places,
And tied on their napkins of cobwebby laces,
The witch served them each
With a howl and a screech,
And they slurped as they filled up their horrible faces.

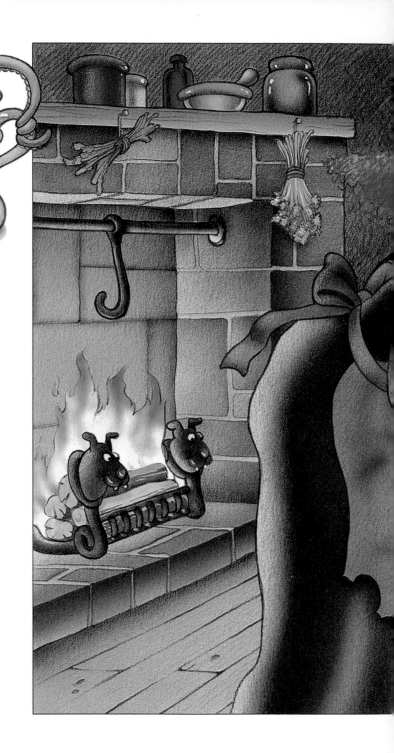

4

The dragon was first to get sick, was he,
Then the rats, snakes and bats
And the chimpanzee,
The spiders went plop,
As the toads fell on top,
Tipping over the cauldron of Gadzook tea.

Weeks later they woke up and growled, "Your tea's
The worst thing you've made us since Scrambled Fleas!"
The witch blushed bright red,
"Why, thank you!", she said,
"I'm so glad you liked it. I try to please."

"Do make it again!" they all yelled with a roar,
"It was so disgusting!", they cried, "We want more!"
 She brewed up a lot, They each drank a pot,
"Enjoy!", shrieked the witch as they sank to the floor.

The witch never lacks now for company,
Her neighbors moved in with her, one, two, three…
Just go by some night,
You'll hear shrieks of delight
As they guzzle down gallons of Gadzook Tea.

Tea End

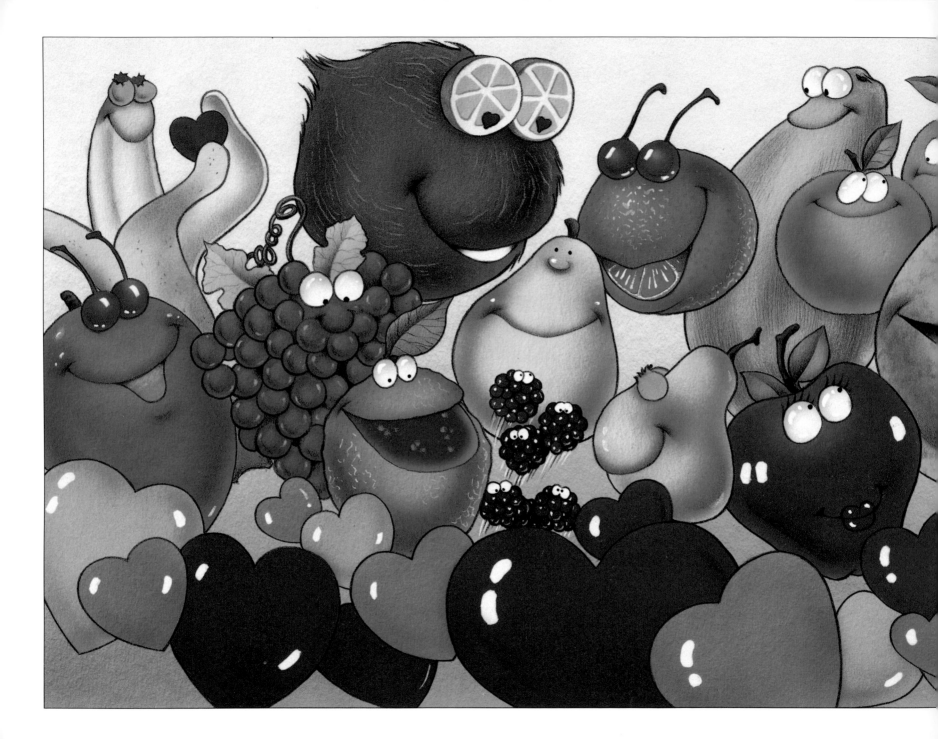

TUTTI FRUTTI LOVESONG

You are my darling CUMQUAT,
Oh, you're my PEACHy pie,
I think you are the BERRIES,
The APPLE of my eye.

Don't make me MELON-choly,
Please be my HONEY DEW,
'Cause oh, my sweet PAPAYA.
I'm BANANAS over you!

I would be oh, so GRAPEful
If you'd just say you care,
For it takes two to MANGO,
And we're a PEACHy PEAR.

Oh, ORANGE you a little
COCONUTS for me too?
Please say you'll be mon CHERRY,
I'm so GUAVA over you.

*HANDY FOOTNOTE

I wrote a note to my Right Foot,
Inviting it to tea,
And when my Left Foot heard the news,
It got mad at me.
"Just because I'm never Right…"
It told me with a pout,
"Is no reason you should go
And make me feel Left out!"

*Well, I have learned a lesson,
To keep a feud from brewing,
I never let my Left Hand
Know what my Right Hand's doing.

10

First Halloween On Mars
(On the occasion of the invasion of Earthlings)

I'm not answering my front door,
Not getting scared like I got before...
A creature of a shape and size
And color I don't recognize
Is jumping out before my eyes
And hollering "Trick or treat!"

My antennae are frazzled through and through,
My wings are sagging, my horns are too,
My heads are aching, my eyes are sore,
My tails cannot wag anymore,
Be still my hearts!...Just hear them beat
Whenever "IT" yells "Trick or treat!"

There goes the doorbell...I'll just peek,
Oh, no!...it has just ONE head...EEEK!
It's bare, without one single scale,
Or one antenna, wing or tail,
And just two arms and just two feet,
And one mouth hollering "Trick or treat!"

Oh, won't this nightmare ever end?
What I need most now is a friend,
Someone normal, just like me,
With three heads where three heads should be,
Right above its ten big feet,
And not hollering, "Trick or treat!"

MUM'S THE WORD

I bought a Mum plant at the store,
The best I'd ever seen,
Its stems were straight,
Its roots were strong,
Its leaves were thick and green.
I kept it moist,
I gave it light,
I did all that I could,
To help my Mum grow big and bright,
The way a mum plant should.
I sang it songs,
I told it tales,
I did not leave its side,
I talked,
    And talked,
        And talked,
            Until
It got so bored it died!

*Published in February, 1991, National Wildlife Federation's Ranger Rick magazine.

14

BEDTIME STORY

So you want a story,
You want me to tell
Of the awful Lump-Bumps
Who dwell down a well?
To tell of the Nasties
That eat everyone,
And to please make it scary,
Because it's more fun!
You want me to tell
Of the Crawlies that creep,
Of the Brawlies that keep you
From falling asleep?
So you want a good fright
And a nice chill or two?...
Well, how about if
I just simply say
BOO!

JILLY JANET KELLY
(A jump rope rhyme)

Jilly
Janet Kelly
Had a dilly
Of a bean,
And she put it
In her pocket
So to keep it
Nice and clean!
Now that Jilly
Janet Kelly's
Bean was made of
Jilly Jelly —
'Twas a dilly,
Of a Jilly
Janet Kelly
Jelly bean!

NOAH'S WIFE

After she scrubbed down the walls,
Swabbed the decks and swept the stalls,
Cleaned the windows, waxed the rails,
Starched and ironed all the sails,
Pulled the mizzenmast up high,
Hung out all the wash to dry,
Made the beds for sleep that night,
Made the Ark all shiny bright,
What did Mrs. Noah do,
When on board came, two by two,
Lions, tigers, birds and monkeys,
Squirrels, elephants and donkeys,
Cows and frogs and kangaroos,
Leaping, kicking, mooing moos…
Pushing, squshing, scrapping, squalling,
Neighing, braying, caterwauling,
 Leaving a great big mess behind,
Didn't Mrs. Noah mind?

Did she cry, "Whoa! I quit!
Really, Noah, this is it!
The swine are pigs!
The snakes are vipers!
The baby elephants need diapers!
The mice are rats!
The snails are slugs!
The bees and fleas just drive me bugs!"
And on and on,
From dawn to dark,
Until poor Noah parked the Ark?

SAME DIFFERENCE

Little wee Lee Lolly Lynne,
Has a sister, Lou, her twin,
Dressed the same,
From head to toes,
Which is Lee?
Which Lou?
Who knows?

Lee looks lovely,
So does Lou,
But I can't tell
Who is who,
Till I meet them
Both and say:
"Hi! How are
You two today?"

When one says:
"Good as can be!"
And one says:
"Don't bother me!"
Then I know
Just who is who…
The nice one's Lee,
The grouch is Lou!

WHEN MAMA COOKS

When Mama cooks a stew for us,
She always makes a lot,
She likes to throw all sorts of things
Into a big, black pot.
She adds some gloop, she adds some glop,
She adds a bunch of gross,
Then
Bubble,
Bobble,
Bibble,
Boil!
She adds another dose.
And very soon it starts to smell
So yummy and delitch,
That's when we are the gladdest that
Our Mama is
A witch!

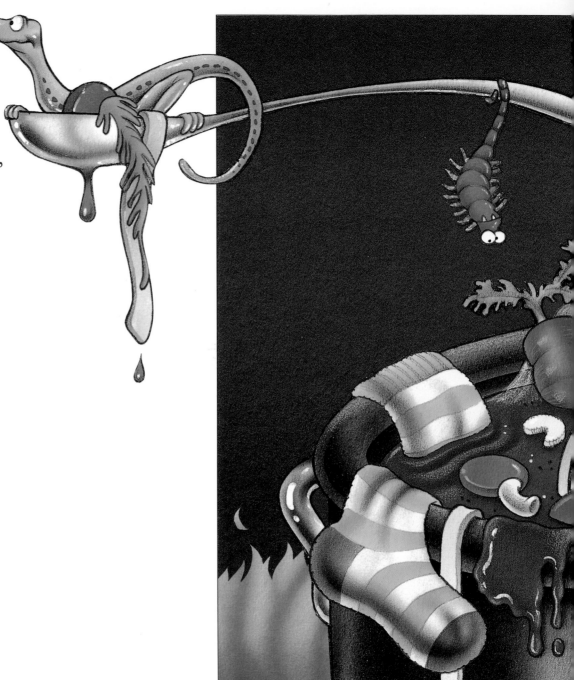

My brother likes butter,
While I prefer batter
My brother eats butter
With bread, but no matter,
My mother eats batter
With bread, but no butter,
And then there's my father
Who goes even further…
 My father eats butter
With big globs of batter,
(He'd eat it with bread but
'Twould make father fatter.)
So, all day we battle,
Each one with the other,
About which is better,
Bread, batter or butter.

INVITATION

If you like your eggs all runny,
If you like toast charcoal brown,
Come to my house, my dad's cooking,
'Cause my mom is out of town.

If you like your white socks colored,
If you like clothes with a streak,
Bring your laundry, my dad's washing,
'Cause my mom's been gone a week.

All our sinks are piled with dishes,
And we've burned up all our pans,
And we're eating with our fingers,
And we're drinking coke from cans.

And we're having week old pizza
For our lunch and dinner too,
But our dad, (who is a health nut),
Makes us scrape off the green goo.

If you like watching t.v. late
And no scolding when you're bad,
Better come before my mom's home,
She's not half as fun as dad.

CONTRARY MARY

Inside she's a Gypsy girl,
Outside, soft and sweet,
Inside she is whacky, wild,
Outside prim and neat,
Inside she's a dinosaur,
Outside, just a puppy,
Inside she's a tiger-shark,
Outside, just a guppy...
But be careful,
Lest she pout
And turns herself
Inside out!

SWEET DREAM

I dreamed up a grandma
All plumpy and sweet,
Who loved to bake brownies
That I loved to eat.
She'd let me taste anything
That she was cooking
And slipped me some nickels
When no one was looking.
She'd always stick up for me
In times of trouble.
And though I just loved her,
She'd love me back double.
She'd always be there for me
Asking "What's new?"
And there wasn't anything
She wouldn't do
To comfort or cheer me up
On a hard day,
To her I was perfect,
In every which way.
I dreamed up this grandma
And suddenly knew
It wasn't a dream,
Grandma dear,
It was you.

A Day In The Life Of Bryant The Giant

Bryant awakes and he stokes up the sun,
Takes a bath in the ocean
And after he's done,
He tramps to his kitchen and starts to beat
A thousand scrambled eggs to eat.
Then off he goes on his daily stroll,
Ten giant steps and he's reached the Pole,
Splashing his way through icy seas,
He crosses the Alps and the Pyrenees,
Puffing his pipe as he lumbers by,
Blowing huge clouds across the sky.
Next, a left turn, and he's trudging south
Straightening swamps and jungles out,
Brushing off lions and tigers who feel
A big, burly giant would make a great meal.

Soon it gets late...night has begun
With one mighty puff, he blows out the sun,
Pins up the moon, straightens the stars
And planets, like Pluto and Venus and Mars.
Once 'round the world he goes and then
Bryant, the Giant, is home again,
Eats fifty pizzas with peppers and cheese,
And, for dessert, ten banana fruit trees.
With one giant yawn, along about ten,
He gets in pajamas and washes up, then,
Leaving his clothes in a big, giant heap,
He jumps into bed with a big giant leap,
Falls fast asleep in his big, giant lair,
With a big giant hug
For his toy teddy bear.

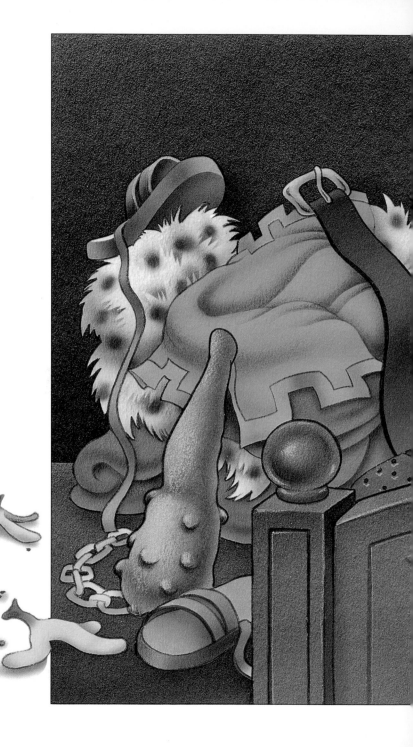

"Wow, Blanche!" Zaza said again. They sang "For She's a Jolly Good Fellow!" and pulled Blanche into a dance.

Even Eva forgot her disappointment that Blanche would not be a great actress at the Farm Theater.

"You never told me you could paint like this!" she said.

"I wasn't sure I could, myself," said Blanche.

"And, by the way, you are no longer shy," Eva observed.

"No," said Blanche. "I am an artist."

The family was amazed.

"These are masterpieces!" Bruno declared. "At last, our plays will have the scenery they deserve!"

"What a talent you have," said Edwin.

So Blanche tried her hand at the sets. She had never painted such big pictures before. First she made little sketches in her book.

Then she copied them onto huge flats.

Days later, when she had finished, she was very pleased.

"I think we should let her try painting the sets," said Edwin.

"I do too," said Sarah.

"Well, *we* are certainly lousy at set painting," said Zaza.

"My, my," Sophie said at last.

"Wow, Blanche," Zaza said. "What a great performance!"

"If only you could do that on stage," said Bruno.

"You're right," said Sophie. "We were not fair to you."

"JUST A MINUTE!" she shouted. "YOU WANT ME TO SHOW MY FEELINGS? WELL, HERE THEY ARE! I FEEL BAD WHEN I CAN'T LEARN TO ACT! I FEEL BAD WHEN I SPILL THE TICKETS! I FEEL BAD WHEN I CAN'T BORROW PROPS FROM STRANGERS! BUT YOU AREN'T FAIR! I DRAW AND PAINT VERY WELL! I CAN MAKE WONDERFUL SETS FOR YOUR PLAY!"

She wandered backstage until she heard voices. When she walked into the room, she heard Zaza say, "Uh oh."

The family was painting sets for the new play. Nothing looked real, and there was lots of spilled paint.

"Blanche, dear," said Sophie. "Where are the props?"

"Your neighbor didn't know who I was," said Blanche. "She thought it was a joke."

"Oh, brother," said Zaza to Sarah. "She is utterly useless!"

"Excuse me," said Blanche. "You know, I'm sure I could paint good sets for you. Then you could spend your time rehearsing."

Bruno said, "Blanche, we are all very sorry. But it has not worked out, having you at the theater...."

"We are sending you back home, dear," said Sophie.

Blanche stared at them. Then, inside her, something exploded.

Blanche took a deep breath and blurted, "I want a rocking horse, a washtub, and a tuba."

There was a pause and then the voice replied, "If this is a practical joke, child, it isn't funny!" The door shut in Blanche's face.

Blanche was completely miserable. If anything else went wrong she didn't think she could bear it! Now she would have to admit that she had failed at props, too.

The countryside was perfectly beautiful! On another day she'd have drawn a picture of it. But now she had an important job! She came to a house and raised her hand to knock, but she just couldn't do it. Then the door flew open.

"I thought someone was there," said a voice. "Are you lost?"

"First she can't act," grumbled Zaza. "Then she can't sell tickets."

"What *can* she do?" said Sarah.

"Everyone is good at something!" said Sophie.

"*I* know!" cried Edwin. "She can collect props for me!"

"PROPS?" asked Blanche.

"Things the actors need for the play," Edwin explained. They told Blanche to go next door and borrow a rocking horse, a washtub, and a tuba.

"ALL RIGHT," said Blanche.

The ticket booth was perfect. She sat on a little chair, out of sight.

Suddenly an unfamiliar voice boomed over her head.

"Excuse me, Miss. I need tickets for opening night!"

Blanche was startled out of her wits.

"HOW MANY?" she said at last.

"Speak up!" bellowed the stranger. "I can't hear you!"

Blanche was so flustered that she upset the box of tickets.

"What's going on?" said Sarah.

"It's true," said Sarah.

Blanche looked out at the family, and she could see that they had all given up on her. She wanted more than anything in the world to be part of this lively group, but they didn't want her at all! She ran out of the theater to find a place where she could be alone.

Bruno whispered, "I'm afraid Blanche will never be an actress."

"I know," said Sophie. "Some people just don't belong on the stage."

Bruno was worried. "What will we tell Eva?"

"Maybe she needs a little more time," said Sophie.

"She has *had* time," said Zaza. "She stinks!"

"Let's pretend that you are the duchess in the play," Sarah began. "I will be the maid, and I will serve you the strange pudding."

"_{OKAY}," said Blanche.

"Take a bite," said Sarah.

Blanche pretended to take a bite of the pudding.

"You are not *acting*," said Sarah. "Show us how it tastes." Blanche took another bite.

"Show us your *feelings*!" cried Sarah. "Watch how I do it." Sarah took a bite of pudding. "*Blaaaaaaaaaaahhhhhhhhhp*! See? Now the audience knows the pudding is strange."

Blanche tried to do what Sarah had done. But she felt much too embarrassed.

Outside, Sarah was sawing boards
for the duchess's bed.

"That Blanche is hopeless!" Zaza
told her.

"What a shame," said Sarah. "She
is so nice."

"Well, I don't think she has any
talent," said Zaza.

"*I* will try teaching her!" said
Sarah.

Blanche felt terrible. She tried to be brave.

When Sarah came in to give her another lesson, Blanche was ready to
try again.

"Oh, dear," said Zaza. She explained that actors must speak so that the audience can hear. In this scene, the actor must show that the maid is angry when the duchess calls her pudding strange. They tried again. Blanche continued to shake and speak in a tiny whisper.

"For heaven's sake, Blanche!" Zaza said. She stormed off the stage.

Blanche opened her sketchbook. A quick drawing always helped when she felt bad.

"*Lackadaisica!*" said Zaza in a loud, bossy voice. "Please explain the meaning of this strange pudding!"

Blanche stared at Zaza.

"Blanche! It's your turn to say your line now," said Zaza in her regular voice.

"IT IS A PERFECTLY NORMAL PUDDING," read Blanche.

Blanche's legs began to shake.

"Take a deep breath," said Zaza. "It's natural to feel nervous at first." Zaza handed her a script. "You are Lackadaisica, the maid. I am the duchess. You have served me a strange pudding.

The next day, the family rehearsed *The Strange Pudding* and Blanche watched. She loved the way Zaza screamed when the pudding jiggled and the way Edwin jumped when it spilled.

Then Zaza said, "Come on, Blanche, it's time for your acting lesson. We can perform a scene from the play."

"What are you carrying?" asked Edwin.

Blanche blushed. "JUST MY SKETCHBOOK," she said.

"Perhaps Zaza could work with Blanche," Sophie said. "She can be an excellent teacher when she puts her mind to it."

Zaza was not thrilled, but she agreed.

"May I look at your sketches?" Edwin whispered to Blanche. She shook her head. "She *is* very shy," Edwin thought.

"ʜᴇʟʟᴏ," said Blanche.

"What did she say?" asked Zaza.

"She said, 'Hello,'" said Eva. "Speak up, Blanche, dear."

Blanche took a deep breath, opened her mouth wide, and said, "ʜᴇʟʟᴏ." She was an only child and was used to spending most of her time alone. She wanted to tell everyone how much she loved the theater, but the words would not come out.

"How delightful, how kind," said Eva. "As it happens, Blanche is with me, in the car. She is a little shy."

"Oh, brother," said Zaza to Sarah. "And she wants to act?"

"Come, Blanche," coaxed Eva. "Come say hello."

"Welcome, dear Eva," said Bruno. "What brings you here?"

"I have a favor to ask of you," said Eva.

"Of course!" cried Bruno. He would never forget that Eva had given them their curtain and box seats.

"I have a young grandchild called Blanche," explained Eva. "I think she is stagestruck. May she come here for a while and learn the craft of acting?"

"We would be honored," said Bruno.

"Why, it's Eva!" cried Sophie. "She used to be an actress long ago.
When we turned the farm into a theater, she was such a help!"

At the Farm Theater, Bruno, Sophie, Zaza, Sarah, and Edwin were having a barbecue to celebrate the final performance of their latest hit, *The Evil Spell*. The very next day they would begin rehearsing Bruno's new play, *The Strange Pudding*.

"Look, someone's coming," said Sarah, "...in a snazzy car."

The Strange Pudding
Opens Soon

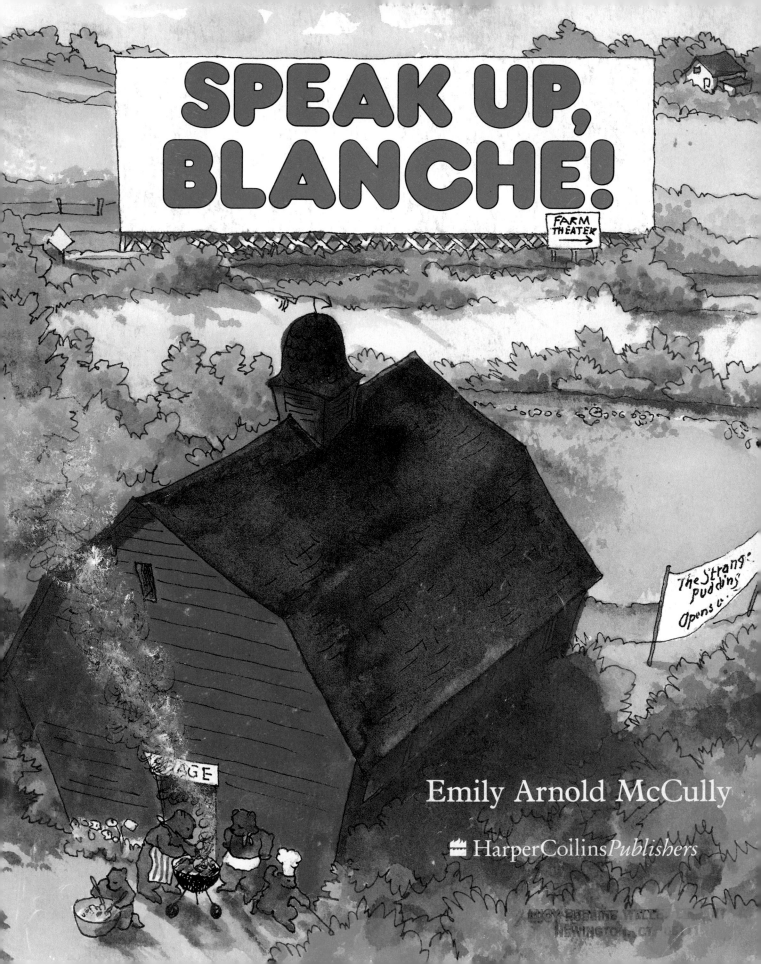

For Jolly and Alfred

Library of Congress Cataloging-in-Publication Data

McCully, Emily Arnold.
    Speak up, Blanche! / Emily Arnold McCully.
        p.   cm.
    Summary: Stagestruck Blanche would like to be a part of a
theatrical bear troupe's new play, but her shyness causes problems
until she discovers a special talent of her very own.
    ISBN 0-06-024227-2. — ISBN 0-06-024228-0 (lib. bdg.)
    [1. Theater—Fiction. 2. Bashfulness—Fiction. 3. Artists—
Fiction. 4. Bears—Fiction.] I. Title.
PZ7.M478415Sp 1991   90-36945
[E]—dc20   CIP
                                                              AC